SCHOOLED FOR LIFE

Other books by the author

Poetry

Robe Of Skin
Milesian Fables
Out Of Exile
Cat Kin
Safe Levels
Living Jazz
Beautiful Is Enough
Omnibus Occasions
Selected Poems 1956-96
Skeleton Keys
Judging By Disappearances
Unholy Empires
Haiku Of Five Decades
Haiku At Seventy
Getting On: Poems 2000-2012

Novels

The Summer Ghosts
Zones
A Sleeping Partner
Strange Alphabet
The Stump
Instrument Of Pleasure
The Drive North
Last Throes
Scrubbers

Non-Fiction

Jean Rhys revisited
Jean Rhys Afterwords

Translations

Maldoror & Complete Works (Lautréamont)
Days And Nights (Jarry)
Flesh Unlimited: Three Novels (Apollinaire & Aragon)
Masochism In America (MacOrlan)
Surrealist Games (Breton, Eluard etc)
Heliogabalus (Artaud)
The Nun (Péret)

SCHOOLED FOR LIFE

ALEXIS LYKIARD

All rights reserved. No part of this work covered by the copyright herein may be reproduced or used in any means – graphic, electronic, or mechanical, including copying, recording, taping, or information storage and retrieval systems – without written permission of the publisher.

Printed by imprintdigital
Upton Pyne, Exeter
www.imprintdigital.net

Typeset by narrator
www.narrator.me.uk
info@narrator.me.uk
033 022 300 39

Published by Shoestring Press
19 Devonshire Avenue, Beeston, Nottingham, NG9 1BS
(0115) 925 1827
www.shoestringpress.co.uk

First published 2015
© Copyright: Alexis Lykiard
www.alexislykiard.com

The moral right of the author has been asserted.

ISBN 978-1-910323-41-0

AUTHOR'S NOTES AND ACKNOWLEDGEMENTS

This new collection is concerned with outgrowing, surviving and trying to transcend, or even learn from, a variety of educational disciplines and experiences. In *A Case Of Samples* (1956), Kingsley Amis – in my view a better poet than novelist – remarks how "Docility, of feature or of mind, /Is glad to wither when the tongue is free". His poem *Lessons* also concludes that "... out of school, all ways the hand will move,/Forget the private hour, and touch the world..." The writer seems here to sound a belated cautionary note to teacher and pupil alike, greeting with wry relief the end of restriction and restraint, yet also aware that there may be much that all of us eventually need to unlearn.

Sicut serpentes sicut columbae.... Wise serpents or docile doves? What *did* our education actually teach us? At any rate, none of the names and initials in *Schooled For Life* have been changed in order to protect anyone, 'innocent' or not, and the memories are as accurate as this septuagenarian can still recall and describe. A 1998 letter from my school contemporary, the late John Moat – who 30 years previously originated The Arvon Foundation – notes that in a prose autobiographical piece introducing my *Selected Poems 1956-1996*, the "only omission [was] those infernal outdoor bogs by the clock-tower – the first year you weren't allowed to close the door for a crap." A detail I'd forgotten, evidently not conducive to poetic treatment then or now!

My thanks to the writer friends, magazine editors and colleagues who first published several of these poems in earlier, often very different versions: Kevin Bailey, Ken Clay, Alan Dent, John Lucas, Stephen Middleton and Tony Simpson, and to *Crazy Oik*, *Haiku Quarterly*, *Mistress Quickly's Bed*, *Ostinato*, *Penniless Press*, *Shoestring Press*, *The Spokesman*.

CONTENTS

Introductory   1

1. Early Learning   3

    English Language Course For Beginners   5
    Hermeneutic   7
    Cutting A Rug   9
    1948   11
    Kept In   13
    Religious Instruction   16
    Mens Sana In Corpore Sano   17
    Public School Codes   19
    Chaps In Chapel   20
    An Aesthetic Education   22
    Top Of Our Class   24
    Old School Ties   26
    Three Haiku   27

2. Better Late Than Never   29

    Forms And Classes   31
    Revaluation In The Poets' Pub   33
    On Track, Off Course   34
    Creative Market Place   34
    Honeyed Words   34
    Past The Education Block   35
    Two Creative Writing Groups   36
    Confucian Precepts For Chinese Travellers   38
    Two Tutorials   39
    Master Of His Arts   41
    An Ancient Alumnus   42
    'On Earth As It Is –'   42
    Now And Then   43
    Slow Learning Fuse   44

INTRODUCTORY

Désormais que ma muse, aussi bien que mes jours,
Touche de son déclin l'inevitable cours,
Et que de ma raison le flambeau va s'éteindre,
Irai-je en consumer les restes à me plaindre?
                    La Fontaine: *Poésies Mêlées*

Reading a few wise words found in an ancient book –
who bothers now with verse? – by La Fontaine,
I followed the French fabulist's advice and took

a long look at my schooling in both joy and pain.
If life then seemed unfair, fools only should complain;
age may bring some relief at not being young again.

1. Early Learning

"Religion, I assert, is like a school tie tied round a pair of white flannels – if it is tight, it is uncomfortable; and if it is loose, you might as well have none at all."
(The 16 year old Malcolm Lowry, writing from The Leys School, Cambridge to a girlfriend, 1926)

ENGLISH LANGUAGE COURSE FOR BEGINNERS

(1946)

First day at day school,
in the Morning Break, I broke
my arm – Sod's Law

not God's – but hard lines
for a six year old Greek lad,
lucky refugee.

Brittle-boned, I guessed
my new British friends were gone
with the Kentish wind.

I'd stay bed-bound, months
on end, stuck in hospital –
Gravesend, then Surrey.

Splints, ops, bone-setting
botched, X-rays, orthopaedics.
A signed plaster-cast.

Little else the Past
(those sorry old times of youth
often still rankling)

offers me now. One learned
the hard way, copper-plate script
left-handed always

despite the fractures.
I grew to love this process
of shifting strange sounds

onto paper, shapes
that made up patterns, meanings
like notes of music

set in their own form,
fitting neatly. They'd not trip
nor fall like I did,

when, as lapsed Stoic,
my first words to the doctor
had been "I suffer".

HERMENEUTIC

(1948-57)

"Sending children to boarding-school at the age of eight is not the only aspect of upper-class Edwardian parenting which seems now to belong to a lost world."
[Jane Stevenson – *Edward Burra: Twentieth-Century Eye*, 2007]

Just who learned *what*, or what was taught to *whom*,
is hard in Twenty-Fourteen to assess. Before
my memories fade or I am made to leave the room
– before I grow hazy and mumble
before I go crazy and crumble –
I might review my English education,
stray bits of it at least, with hindsight, fits of gloom
or humour. No further cause for trepidation,
dread of some threat or sharp reprisal if one
balked at what Authority deemed gospel truth....
A stolid gamesmanship seemed fittest way through life.

Reflection's how age comes to terms with youth:
boarding-school boys played dumb, young puppets when
harangued, silenced by ancient, arbitrary rules
applied to athletes, swots, neat sycophants and fools
alike. All learned exam techniques, and not much more:
essays scored Alpha Plus to Delta, but by then
most of us were definitively marked for life.

Nonsense reigned supreme, like weirdness on the wireless.
Take *Educating Archie*, an absurd half-hour,
Light Programme-style – strange stuff that starred bland Peter Brough,
ventriloquist! And Andrews, A., homunculus,
crude wooden imp in shorts, possessed of freakish power,
whose chirpy cheek would always prompt his mentor's tight

-lipped frown. Uniformed captives, we ourselves weren't quite
as quick with smart-arse answers; hour by leaden hour,
dummies colluded, quiet, well-trained. Was it enough,
waiting one's cue, to get the promised best of life?

CUTTING A RUG

> *Cut A Rug.* To 'jive' or 'jitterbug': dance addicts: adopted from US soldiers in 1943.
> Eric Partridge: *A Dictionary Of Slang* (1982 edn.)

Was it some kind of record? My first day
at boarding-school, aged eight, taught me a thing
or two about obedience, the church,
justice and so on, but you don't complain
about the status quo – you're stuck with that.
I knew how homesick, foreign, oddly named
and scared I was: you simply frowned, the pain
was nothing to admit. But why should I
have done the surreal deed of which I stood
accused? Unthinkable! Sheer pointlessness
denying crime, though, and my protests did no good
under the circumstances. I'd been framed
and never in my schooldays found out why.

Horribly flexible, the slippers used
for beating boasted half-inch rubber soles.
You bent bare-bottomed by the bed while he,
Headmaster Reverend Aubrey Hooper, swung
hard, wholly unerring as to aim, and
skilful enough to make small buttocks sting.
The situation as I saw it then –
undignified, daft, laughable, unfair –
might not have altered radically with time:
you get to know the score. *To take a pair
of scissors and deliberately destroy
the fringe of Jackson Major's blanket, well,
sinful behaviour's punished in a boy,
six strokes for that.* Prep school did not prepare
me to engage so promptly with the absurd,
fierce eccentricities of life, though Hell
was just an alien notion I soon turned down flat.
The following day I forced a smile, when word

went round my disbelieving peers how I
was beaten for a novel crime, *cutting a rug*.
Can you beat that? They couldn't. I'd enjoy
friends, games, orthodox lessons (more or less),
hot summer days that cannot burn again.
Everyone wondered why I'd vandalize
an older boy's bedding, yet the pattern's clear
enough. Memory folds a bluegreen tartan
into place, pristine, intact and neat as
myself then. Holding fast under duress,
hedonist Greek, I feigned becoming Spartan
until my time was right, when to cut loose
was paradise.
                I'd laugh for real, amused
to find words wouldn't leave me in the lurch.
Language and jazz and women – my loves fused,
seeming to hint, via that great Ellingtonian's band,
how jovial pleasure, art, time's subtle beat,
might all meet and endure, many years on:
Cootie Williams & His Rug Cutters. They
play now, and for the record I am grateful, gone.

1948

Curious preponderance of memories
from prep school days, nutty professors plus a clutch
of superannuated military men
who struggled to impose some discipline
in those glum, straitened postwar years.
What a fraternity of oddbods, solemn priests,
grizzled and scarlet drunks whose threadbare
rearguard mission – generally thwarted – was to catch
us out and punish misdemeanours! Our egregious
errors in Maths or Latin Grammar underlined
a shameful failure for our teachers.... Who return,
flaunting their varied yet distinct absurdity,
if not in nightmare, then via convoluted narratives –
strange but quite whimsical projections, men with zany
mannerisms, tics of speech or body, weird behaviour –
deceptive traces of that long-gone decade.
Now that I know I'm old myself, the film
I watch increasingly, in all its faded monochrome,
holds some hilarious if horrific interest....
Witness: blunt and sharp objects hurled across
classrooms, blackboard dusters and protractors
angrily aimed by our short-tempered masters.
One fellow twisted hair on youthful napes;
another, teaching music, would half-turn
casually from the keyboard, sliding fingers
alongside boys' bare knees and up their shorts.
Dismayed, we warned each other, backed away; a few
might even have sidled nearer the old upright,
to tease those prancing digits. Nobody sneaked,
at any rate; you just dropped out, could choose
not to learn scales and staves and notes and all
that dreary nonsense, bafflingly suspect.
Concocting japes at end of term was ace:
the farting contests always prompted adult pique –
sarcastic thunder, or some wondrous burst of rage –
everyone on Detention, class closed down,

writing of endless lines on sunny afternoons.
The rarest fun was when one nerve-wracked pedagogue
became exasperated, ducking out
in panic: such a hasty exit meant we'd won
(door slammed to an accompaniment of cheers).
I understand now what they taught us then
during those latter days of rationing,
lessons both piffling and profound, extremes
that often seemed to meet. Confusion reigned
all round at boarding school in 1948,
my own eighth year – a misty time now grown
curiously full of powdered eggs and whalemeat,
unappetising food of every kind. (At least
it wasn't Greece – nobody starved!)
A time for feeling small and alien, most alone,
adapting to new rituals, day by day,
desperate to fit in, own up, and accept my fate.
Despite myself, I learned a lot although
I scarcely understood a thing…. Those times,
elusive yet recurrent, slow to fade away,
aren't so disturbing to return to – younger days
of '48, remembered rather as dark grey,
exhaustingly austere, too drab for love or hate.

KEPT IN

[The names are the same, their owners long dead;
they bafflingly came to live on in my head.]

Gripped by one ear, marched back to the Nineteen
Forties, I'm compelled to stay on at my desk.
Here, until lines are done, I must remain,

detention-stranded.... Fearful rebels we all felt,
Viyella-hairshirted penitents. Our flannel shorts
stayed up via serpent-clasp elastic belt

worn with black indoor-shoes, elastic-panelled too.
Uniform drabness, from school cap to stockings,
marked the vile kit.... Weirdest arcana we were taught

by those moustachioed haughty masters who
challenged us to combat – a grave trio of tall
overseers, grey gargoyles awkward in recall.

Roll Call has echoes though: they're soon lined up again
and fill my daydream, three old guys, grotesque
uneasy martinets, not men of Alamein.

Colonel Rudgard, Major Mallock, Captain Bent –
officers in pecking-order might pull rank
inter se quite smartly; here one learned odd things!

The seedy Captain liked a drink, seemed prone to swank.
The rakish, mincing Major kept us steering clear
of close-shaved grass, immaculate flowerbeds.

Across my essay, Rudgard in red biro drew
the neatest Pluto creature. A balloon of Z's
rose sizzling from its nose. The caption read:

Lazy Hound! 'Handlebars' the Captain had. He stank
of gin and Craven A's. Utterly slewed one night,
he left his baby Austin on the school's front

lawn; both its muddy doors hung shameless in a yawn.
None witnessed this sad, sodden flight – when Captain Bent
went AWOL, tired perhaps of fighting the good fight

and having a dull priest like our stern Head berate
him; those were grimmer days of Bible-bashing rage,
rants at 'self-abuse', acts of a bibulous bent.

Mutiny simmered too within the Colonel's class:
Stevenson, read aloud, he deemed a splendid treat
at End-of-Term. I quite enjoyed an R.L.S

yarn – stylish, exciting, not a bit effete –
yet Rudgard wore 'the walrus fringe', a yellow mess!
We smoother lads would give him lip, quick at our age

to blow away old farts…. It wasn't subtle stuff –
volleys of bad air from each cheeky arse,
saw off Blind Pew and sank the Colonel too.

Foe of afflatus, arty Rudgard forced a cough,
threatened, then bellowed. Nobody, for once, owned up.
More loud reports. Until he'd stood enough,

and stormed out, vowing to thrash every young pup
who messed about. "Bags I first go to walk the plank"
cried one wit: "Shipmates beware of my rear gun!"

Thus Colonels crack up, broken by mere wind….
Mallock we (as it were) let off: figure of fun,
whose own fine airs no bugler could affect to hate,

he was our classmate P.J. Mallock's dapper dad.
The Major's 'toothbrush', tweezer-trimmed, looked cute
with winsome trilby, hirsute tweeds – no hint of mad

unruliness, nor drooling fetish to sustain….
The proper war? Our martial threesome never went
through it – age sidelined Mallock, Rudgard, Bent.

New troops of ruined boys fall in now, older soldiers gone,
the desks all shrunk and cracked. None can explain
that yearning, drunken urge to cut a dash, act tough,

showing our elders we see through their threadbare con.
Meanwhile the late bell sounds. Each fool scrawls on in vain.
Time's up. Hand in this prep school sketch, however rough.

RELIGIOUS INSTRUCTION

Just as well the Bishop was of Winchester
not Birmingham. Most prep school lads became aware
of that lewd limerick about the latter –
where one line rhymed *confirming 'em*. Yet who would dare
smirk out of turn? We bowed heads and devoutly knelt
in a submissive row to be received
into the C of E. Our grim Headmaster
had catechised us thoroughly by then:
sick of those endless Qs and As, I felt
welcome relief. That strange stuff parroted by rote –
cue for an enigmatic, reverential rite –
could be forgotten at long last! *Amen*
sounded a brief spell against Sin. Young souls were saved.
Or not. Fuck knows what any twelve year old believed.

MENS SANA IN CORPORE SANO

A Church of England vicar, our Headmaster,
taught us classics and scripture – OT and NT.
I have described him elsewhere, sometimes recollect
his features and recall that awkward 'Leaver's Talk'
delivered in his study. He urged "Don't defile
the temple of your body. A good Christian won't."
Et cetera…. How come I ended up an atheist?
Did I not muse upon "the dark lasts of the flush",
as a guest preacher sermonized one Sunday
in the nearby village church? Eversley, Hants,
was where Charles Kingsley in Victorian days
wrote worthy, edifying yarns for boys and girls –
Westward Ho!, *The Water Babies* – both were read
as moral works in post-war England. I preferred
Foxe's Book of Martyrs and *The Lancashire
Witches*, perplexing finds in the school library,
weird and gruesome fare for the pubescent mind….
Kingsley, a rather complex country parson –
pedagogue, perhaps a closet paedophile – held
flagellant fantasies and may have mortified
the wayward flesh we were exhorted to eschew.
'Muscular Christianity', the famous phrase
espoused by Anglicans and zealously applied
to children of the Forties, recognized that we,
like our fond parents, reckoned corporal punishment
could well discourage serious misbehaviour.
Our Saviour's own example, Bible-reading hours,
and decent manners, would prepare us best for life.

Matron – Miss Dobinson, gaunt and horse–faced (Dobbin
of course!), her grey hair in the neatest bun,
made sure we all stayed 'regular'. A tick or cross,
entered in her big black ledger every day,
judged whether any laxative would be required.
The constipated bowel might receive
a dose of Scott's Emulsion, Syrup of Figs,

or Milk of Magnesia – what a nauseous choice
was ours! No other female crossed our path
but the Headmaster's wife, elderly too.

Such was the healthy life, the rural setting
wondrously idyllic, where pine-wooded grounds
(with gumboots – never 'wellies' – quintessential)
had rhododendron, adders, easy trees to climb;
escape from cheerless maths or morning prayers, PT
with star-jumps, stretches, running-on-the-spot! Our sweets
were strictly rationed though, as in the world outside:
eight items each, extracted from your Term's supply,
would be doled out twice weekly. Swaps took place –
scrambles for Meltis Berry Fruits or Fox's
Glacier Mints, toffees for bits of Aero, Bassett's
Liquorice Allsorts.... Seventy-odd boarders,
half-a-dozen to a dorm, we liked the summers
best – our school sported a small swimming pool,
while cricket was worth being far from home for.
We invented frisbees too, and long before
somebody made a fortune from them; Primula
cheese, packaged in cardboard circles, served also
as flying saucers – popular obsession then.
Those callow years of youth weren't 'learning curves',
and won't float back; the heaviest lesson simply serves
to tease or puzzle us. Scenes fading past recall
invite some ghostly laughter, matter not at all.

PUBLIC SCHOOL CODES

Loyalty to what is wrong, outmoded, reactionary is mischievous.
(C.L.R. James, *Beyond A Boundary*, 1963)

Sets of notice-board initials, surviving pointlessness,
are simply abstract threats now, scrawls to plague the memory.
Plain versions of their owners' fancier dress,
P.D.L.W, J.V.P.T
once spelled quadruply capital Authority
– plus S.H.P, C.A.L, P.S.C,
black-gowned, three-lettered vampires, vanished yesterday....
Our masters marked us more than canes could. They

stood for hermetic rites: boys had no cause to try
flouting established Law. On which last score,
W.M[cubed], ordained Head, gave devout Reasons-Why,
although his earnest sportsmanship exposed the bore.
God remained cliché, cypher quite the same
as questionable 'A.N. Other' – flippant name
on Team-Lists in the Cloister, pinned head-high –
nothing but teasing guesswork at that sternest Away Game.

CHAPS IN CHAPEL

Half-baked Gothic style, its red brick ornamented
with some ornate tiles and slates.... Not much
in the way of stained-glass worth a mention. Nothing,
aesthetically speaking, to impress
the adolescent – ugly building, uninspired.
Solid mid-Victorian architecture, quite
opulently squat. Wealth aspiring to maintain
and boast its muscular Christianity: fine site
for sons of the – already risen – bourgeoisie.
A collegiate Oxford was what School and Chapel
modelled themselves upon. And so we aped adult
servility, taught to be loyal subjects now
of new young Queen and new, devout Headmaster
himself most recently installed. Obedience
the vital code instilled in us: only to stand
and wait in line; your turn comes round and then you rule.
The seniors of each House, the Prefects,
were ushers as we shuffled past in rowdy file.
Instead of black gowns over tweed-and-flannel
we donned Sunday suits of navy serge – white surplice
de rigueur, to mark an arcane Feast or Saint's Day....
Choristers, churchmen and Authorities
along with privileged sixthformers and House Prefects
were ranked downstairs, seated on either side
of the wide aisle, in smug, unblinking grandeur.
We sullen mid-teen nobodies then pushed and shoved
ascending the stone staircase to the Gallery.
There in long rows of wooden pews we might avoid
closer surveillance; two short-sighted masters sat
at either end. Now we could clown a bit, pass notes,
invent odd pastimes to amuse ourselves.... Some brazen
chaps played chess on miniature boxed sets,
the pieces plugged securely to the board,
stashed with due speed as each longwinded sermon
droned to its dreary end. Then we would stand,
adopt varieties of silly voices

to bellow hymns whose thumping rhymes had catchy tunes.
Onward Christian soldiers marching as to war
With the cross of Jesus going on before....
You used to fidget through slow, futile rituals,
resenting even then the chronicles
of time so eminently wasted; chapel days
seemed lacking purpose, as we gabbled vapid
forms of words: *And our mouths shall show forth thy praise....*
O Lord, make haste to help us.... Such responses
we were trained to give, all mystifyingly
portentous or irrelevant. Most junior boys
knew boarding school regime contrived to mask
injustice, but divined youth was a special age
which, while not golden, held some hidden virtue,
and shouldn't be the passive prey of Holy Joes
conducting their own holy show – an unctuous parade.
Can laughter, love or reason help dispel
unwelcome and enduring memories of such stuff?
Those Jacobeans who translated biblical
myths said not a lot to acned and indifferent lads,
for whom most organ music was a sonorous bore.
Chapel, like Corps, involved just one more drill.
We stood, knelt, sat or genuflected on demand,
checking wristwatches for the umpteenth dismal time,
wishing ourselves whisked by a miracle elsewhere.
This rigmarole, like water-torture, wasn't fair;
being sent away for months on end was punishment
enough.... A few perceptions lingered, wouldn't fade:
to learn there were no gods, no paradise or hell,
meant you might live a free, a sceptic humanist
existence. That, above all, seemed no bad thing,
whatever else one was obliged to chant or sing.
The Truth did not belong to some religionist –
more likely to *all people that on earth do dwell.*
Fate or capricious genes will dole out our few days;
the sole concern is living well. Yet idols cast their spell:
vainly we look skyward, though shadows need no praise.

AN AESTHETIC EDUCATION

    i.m. Gerald Brenan OR, & Peter Cook, OR

Poems and music kept me sane through the winter of '56,
a teenage misfit fallen foul of The Hierarchic Fix.
How odd to hear – same boarding school, next autumn, '57 –
the English master holding forth, as if the place were Heaven.
According to him I'd best stay on, a further sixth-form year
at that school so loathed by writers. Rule of ridicule and fear:
beatings, cold baths and buggery, off to Chapel twice a day.
What bait might there be dangling, what prize to make anyone stay?

The title role was thus proposed, in the annual College Play
which Mr Way directed; as Literature Man, he reckoned
to star a sorry bookworm as the hapless *Edward the Second*.
Did the offer tempt me – perfect shadow in his sunshine day?
A most unusual pedagogue, enthusiast and joker,
Maestro Way thought the play the thing to excite his English class:
Kit Marlowe's ineffectual King ends the bright day with a poker
thrust, heated to vilest effect, up a ringingly blank verse arse….

Here's where Way the intellectual soared seriously out of touch,
fell rather short on casting: with gloomy outsiders like me
noble failure didn't convince. I couldn't interpret such
a subtle atheist view of masochism and monarchy,
but guessed reflected glory's what some teachers can chase after –
applause for them, abuse for you, cat-calls and misplaced laughter.
Rotting in rural jail was enough, why prolong my banishment?
There were plenty more exiled Players trained to imitate young Gent-

-lemen, while rituals of dumb attrition emphasised all that:
early learning made one don a mask, doff cap, and covet hat.
Warped humour may prompt teachers, those who prop up the status quo,
so the Corps, whose C-in-C was Way, staged its own weekly show,
meek squads of regimented kids, gone with the great khaki flow.
None could evade parade drill – scenes of an undramatic kind
that forced us all to enlist in some Theatre of the Absurd.
Why trust any thwarted thesp? Away with Establishment tricks!

Pantomimic, pointless routines exist, and are soon replaced.
The world elsewhere held auditions: actors of all kinds beckoned;
girls in friendly abundance redeemed each wanker – none went blind,
nor plummeted crazy to Hell. Madness meant being absent
from the real and proper action, when time seemed too short to waste.
Our mentors get superseded, but one thought alone occurred
to me – I'd learned enough from books, from boys behaving badly.
The time was ripe to take my leave of privilege and Radley.

TOP OF OUR CLASS

City Pays Tribute To Princess (Headline, *Exeter Leader,* Feb. 2002)

1.

Exonians and ex-forces folk seem none too bright
when it's a question of a new 'Condolence Book'
opened to honour uncrowned head or smiling crook:
Sign Here, endorse the latest right royal parasite!
They serve to exorcise the doubtful past, these glossy shows,
photos already faded of HRH Margaret Rose.

Her legendary rudeness isn't missed:
the plebs had to bow low to this Princess.
She liked to smoke and tipple – but unless
with entertainers, rarely mixed with Jews or blacks.
Lesser mortals might exist, though most crushingly dismissed:
en masse they were simply subjects, who loyally paid tax.

2.

St Peter's College, Radley's Cadet Corps
was both an imposition and a bore.
We'd blanco, brasso, drill in battle dress,
and spit and polish and obsessively
clean each Great War Lee Enfield 303,
we public schoolboys privileged to be
marched along Berkshire small-town streets, saluting the Princess!

One gloomy thought was filling me with dread,
the spectre of conscription – National Service – loomed ahead.
Obliged then to rehearse this futile show,
even at sweet sixteen we came to know
the ways of gentlemen, those lackeys of the press,
whose pack, back in those days, would smartly acquiesce,
praise the Windsor gravy-train…. That unholy regal mess

remained, for some of us, a mystery:
couldn't the British learn from history?
Gawky toy soldiers, khaki-clad, we lined
the streets of Abingdon in 1956,
awkward at attention, impatient yet resigned,
absurd stiff prisoners, a most adolescent mix.
In turquoise coat and pancake makeup, almost mockingly,

a wizened doll strolled past our ranks. As she
processed, she'd glance up now and then, and graciously
bestow a crowning, crimson-lipsticked grin
which gave us all the giggles. (At the gin
again?) This smallscale younger version of the Queen,
everyone later said, was slave to nicotine.
Liquor and shags she liked, though not in that unique.

Hell-bent on holidays, she spent months on Mustique.
Her elder sister's 'New Elizabethan Age',
so loudly heralded four years before,
was reckoned a mirage. Nothing would change.
Why not line up that outworn dynasty
as future targets on our rifle-range?
I daydreamed first her hat might blow away....

3.

Seems only yesterday! The hoariest cliché
remaining half-true, can incite to rage:
*She drank and smoked herself to death for three score years
and ten.* So then, on cue, must we shed servile tears?
Poor old rich biddy, bigoted millionaire,
who on earth laments her? Inheriting their share
of taxfree wealth, those dull fastbreeding Royals
will only party on, on misbegotten spoils.
Within our not-so-sunny isles, nothing shall change.
Reading between Obituary lines, it's clear
the odious Margaret Rose is mourned by sadly few.
Toadying Laureate Odes to her may flow, but here
in colder print's an older, soberer Radleian view.

OLD SCHOOL TIES

> 'Aint never goin back to my old school'
> Steely Dan: *My Old School* (1973)

Sicut serpentes
sicut columbae – Latin
tag wholly obscure

as Christian motto.
Bullies, athletes, sneaks and fools,
arselickers thrived there.

John Moat, Peter Cook –
they and I grew to detest
our *alma mater*.

THREE HAIKU

PURPLE PATCHES

(Impetigo, St Neots, 1950)

Saved from a star role
in the school Christmas play, salved
with gentian violet

EDMUND BLUNDEN'S VISIT

(Radley, 1956)

Bardic survivor,
silver-haired ancient – sixty
to my green sixteen

CAMBRIDGE, 1958

Wintry courtyard where
old Sir John hobbles, hailing
bemused young Kingsmen

2. Better Late Than Never

"No pen, no ink, no table, no room, no time, no quiet, no inclination."
(24 year old James Joyce, writing to his brother, 1906)

FORMS AND CLASSES

A young author, high-flyer once, was sent in the late Seventies
on a mission to educate. Marooned awhile on Mauritius,
should he have guessed how best to please, blithely encourage
    or unfreeze
Workshop Group creativities, by winningly and without fuss
using bookish magic to cite empirical authority?
Weirdly their faces float back, haunt that Brit. Council bratpacker – me.
Where's Dr Christopher Gungah or Mrs Emmeline Yip Tong?
What became of those friendly folk – where on earth do we all belong?
A becalmed multi-coloured band of Indians, Creoles and Chinese,
mild-mannered, mixed-race Francophones, and a handful of Portuguese,
awaited my pearls, patiently. (Thirty-something wisdom-and-wit
from a luckier displaced Greek.) This guest wasn't therefore quite a
true Briton, but misfit rather, wholeheartedly striving to be
greeted as a success of sorts, if not Famous English Writer.

'77 seemed the year of the Dodo, indolent bird,
a *rara avis* long vanished, and hunted down beyond recall
somewhere in that 'overcrowded barracoon' which V.S. Naipaul
had fiercely derided. (These days, a call-centre captive supplies
the "How may I help?"– chirpy tone, disingenuous, if not wise.)
My own place, a plaster archway, held *trompe-l'oeil* on studio wall,
PROFESSOR AT PALACE FAÇADE. A likeness in matt black-
    and-white,
Guru Pose convincing enough…. Thus was answered my photocall,
as the group's photographer readied cumbersome tripod and plate.
A busy Chinese in red silk, she ducked back beneath the black hood:
"*Use mile preez!*"– one uneasily kept a straight authorial face.
The obsolete, cheesy machine ostentatiously shuddered. At last
reluctant, caught almost wincing, I form part of the awkward past.
Are we doomed henceforth to recall those boundless, imperiously white

expanses of sand? Palms that sway on bountiful Paradise Isle
once entranced those wise men of words, Joseph Conrad and
    Baudelaire….
While flâneurs select or ignore what's on lawful offer to view,

plain poverty clearly must scratch angry claw-marks on tourists too.
Let a few scrawny fowls protest. All squawk and flap sharply away
from official black juggernaut, our Union Jack-flying limousine.
Blank stares invariably greet us, mark a sad, apathetic scene,
yet the tepid, tropical stench hits you hard, democratically….
That backwater reeked of despair. There I, half-ensnared by its lack
of verve, had to hear out each gripe; the group felt perplexed by the fact
UK publishers would reject what were largely abortive squibs.
("Sir, won't all this reading dilute my own individual style?")
A grandiose lethargy ruled, talk of fear of 'losing one's knack'.
If Literature cushioned each trip, it should underline how rotten

-ly empires confuse or evolve. Yet while Capitalism's a *word*,
the way it's employed, the gross weight, drives hostages mad in its thrall;
through practices wholly unjust, it persists as evil, absurd,
still avid to carve up small worlds. Since colonial histories
have brought home some shameful defeats, why support this worst
    of all fibs?
(Subtext of lives unexamined, the fate of the deprived.) Swift tongues
entertain in hardest end-times, as on we go squandering words,
dashing carelessly into print. Bloated ego or perished thought
spell cyber-*indignatio* – each click of protest fuels the fray!
So what, if anything, was learnt from that brief sunshine yesterday?
Faded pictures I file away; they were worth a cursory look
at least, along with the remains of one brief long-abandoned book….
We're sold a religion of greed, whose mythical lies, dearly bought,
still consume us. Abused, ill-used, the true life goes on forgotten.

REVALUATION IN THE POETS' PUB

Our Workshop group debates the 'worst Poetic Crime',
bent on linking
offender and sad lines, as hindsight often shows
how some dead versifier ended second-rate.
The bubbles in the glass keep winking,
threaten to spill into most splendid rhyme,
enrich us, help us laugh at penury we chose.
Each vows, mock-serious, to sing and praise perfection,

shun the hour of karaoke, chase perception
until the bland finale – unforgiving Close
of Play. Forget good work, if keen to cultivate
contacts, sell out, or flatter for a fee.
Best stay content to struggle honestly,
enjoying the hard game of poetry....
Careerists all betray their slender gifts. You name
one such who compromised the sacred flame,

was duly celebrated, soon and late.
Born charmer, lovely chap, too smooth to hate –
how fortunate the fellow-travelling apostate
should end up safely Faberized, Possum's old mate!
Ignorant of what cash the CIA
can freely freight the verbal scales with, he drew pay,
scarcely self-questioning: the dull dog had his day.
Thus did a disingenuous, well-connected creep

engender verse whose very bathos might seem deep.
Tall story man or Thirties schoolboy-pretender?
Banal white knight of the soul, Sir Stephen Spender
was a talent surrendered to Caesar, one long lifetime
spent in thinking
*"continually of those
who were truly great."*

ON TRACK, OFF COURSE

In distant days I urged my writing students "Squeeze
    all strong utterance. Use the haiku. These
    forms which seem restrictive can help you
    distil, then free your thought. Calm lines and few."
I've come to wonder if some things I taught were true.

CREATIVE MARKET PLACE

Workshopaholics
'buy into' flashy secrets
of writing Success

HONEYED WORDS

Busy wannabes
suck up the easy instant
tips from doubtful minds

PAST THE EDUCATION BLOCK

(Prison pictures from the 1980s)

Rain had soon lent the compound's red
flagstones a rubbery deceptive shine....
Cons clad in sadly faded blues run
darkened by downpour to the gym
before this rapid cloudburst's done

its worst, made space again for blue.
A fortnight's brief and then I'm through.
Three of my 'regulars' already out.
No cricket played and summer spent
in growing overdraft, deluge of debts,

but few regrets. Books did get written,
poems were read, I shall call back good talk.
It drizzles away.... Until a tall black dude supplies
a *Good Jail Guide*, relaying casual tales
of deaths inside, odd feuds or jokes gone wrong

enough to end in some hothead's demise.
A beefy, panic-stricken 22-year-man,
wife-slaughterer and cannibal,
hastens to confront us, quick to veto photos.
This rather bemuses my guest speaker

the friendly lensman, veteran of Nam,
whose celebrated eye is focussed
on one sunlit workshop with contrasting green
high chainlink fence. And so a shutter clicks
to recollect our borrowed time.

TWO CREATIVE WRITING GROUPS

    Devon, 1980s

1. *Captive Audience*

"A better class
of prisoner here
in our new local open nick"
my host quips as we pass.
They stare at her.
Casually one cups his prick.

Young dopers relish any whiff of farce,
favour her with cynic
grins. Everyone's aware
enough to suss that Art's
an ancient con, a fancy caper, mere
time-displacing trick.

2. Colonial Versifiers

> ... it is always in the name of the easy past that he condemns the difficult present.
> Randall Jarrell: *The Obscurity Of The Poet*

"Why read" (his grin is smug) "this modern stuff?
It all should rhyme.
Kipling's the man for me."
I shrug: one last resort seems fair enough.
"Don't waste group time.
Since I'm ill-paid to be
a literary Aunt Sally here, I'll tough
it out – your crime
is not to know you're free.

So why enlist dead words? They play quite rough,
live poets. I'm
bored with minced history....
Argument's useful, sure, but let's not wank!
Better believe I've called your bluff –
Plath next week." Good ploy that, to lose our crank.

CONFUCIAN PRECEPTS FOR CHINESE TRAVELLERS

Desist from the limp handshake.
Nose-picking in public's a no-no,
So is soiling of the swimming pool.
Remember not to mention Pork.

> [via *Guidebook for Civilised Tourism*,
> 64 pp., issued by the Party, 1st Oct 2013.]

TWO TUTORIALS

(via Senex the Cynic)

1. *On Teachers*

Chaos invests, and then sorely infects, our verbal marketplace:
a sorry confusion of rules results in no mark of disgrace:
you're met with loutish, blank incomprehension
when a trace of mild annoyance is labelled condescension.
The rare outburst of precision, more sharply focussed rage,
is called elitist pedantry, an aberration of old age.
Some phrases though are right, exact – on these we should agree,
ensuring that they are retained. Thus *Between you and me*
is correct ('*if you like*'), but not the grocer's odd apostrophe.
Misleading clichés – *in good faith* or *to be honest* – help us see
how rhetoric often falls short and thought is humour-free.
No-one and *alright* are incorrect, indubitably wrong,
each is one phrase of two words, with neither hyphenated,
and rather few, apparently, reckon upon *decimated*.

Spelling's for purist quibblers, since online you can check and belong;
screens of all kinds blunt most viewers' minds, blurring a partial vision:
so tele and broadband rule, real style becomes *clearly* redundant.
In the internet world anyhow, words grow inert, get misused,
filling pages of jargon while most peergroups will boast abundant
exemplars of simple crudeness which can't easily be excused.
Offenders might once have met with some swift, well-directed *abuse*,
itself both motive and cue for an outraged, curt admonition,
or at least some patient mentor's quip – a quite proper, brisk retort,
firm and yet seen to be fair, of the strictly pedagogic sort.
Feckless, uncaring parents ensure there's no sense of right or wrong,
so oafishness goes unchastised; keep order and add to ennui....
Full marks to beleaguered teachers who cope daily with this rat-race,
trapped in the endless class struggle and doubting their own position.

2. On Pundits

Why should we *meet with* people, and never simply *meet* them?
How come silly pillocks *head up* some spurious group
that will equally, inanely, *talk up* another stup-
id scam? Shall good sense or schooling defeat them?
Must one talk *down* or *dumb down*, and meekly give up the fight?
Now every dunce is equal, nothing's really wrong or right,
none admits error – not bankers, admen, politicians,
fraudulent MPs or swarms of spin-physicians....
They're friendly fellows too, who feed the relentless media:
glib, convincing lobbyists keen to register their trite
blasts of triumphal wind *delivered* in the client's name;
exuding easy bonhomie they mask self-serving missions.
Any words that work will do: propaganda knows no shame;
facile fibs, half-truths or gossip amount to much the same.
Life spells lazy verbiage, but the frantic hunting game
impels our busy PR crowd whose main, obsessive aim
is to grab the bright chimera – Success you don't gainsay.
But revised news, swift *redaction*, vainglory, cloud the day:
clear fact remains extremely dull, plain boring, doesn't pay.
Persuasive ways with words need sterner practice than
the conmen ever countenance; their flawed philosophy
calls for the exercise of charm, persistence, a fat fee.
All's fair in bluff and war – farewell 'accepted' procedure;
dust off the expedient clichés without any jot of shame.
Go for the quick linguistic fix, click on Wikipedia,
deploy duff statistics, doubtful research, since nothing can
puncture the Pundit Role, immune from correction or blame.

MASTER OF HIS ARTS

>i.m. D.J. Enright (1920-2002)

Enright's selected essays from the early
Seventies sport the genial if subacid title *Man
Is An Onion*, proffering a neatly playful
wink at Goethe, Hesse – plus, I guess, a hint
of Ibsen's verse protagonist Peer Gynt.
Savour a batch of past reviews then, short and shrewd,
surveying poetry and prose with irony
and insight. Quite a feast of ambiguity's
gathered here to stimulate those ideal readers
every critic hopes to reach, delight, instruct.
Teacher and poet, scholar, novelist, Enright
set some high standards of plain speech and intellect;
his quizzical enquiries could revaluate
work thought to be enduring or ephemeral.

One may prize the few such sceptic humanists,
who make straight comments without fear or favour.
Never vainglorious, they preserve some cleansing truths
and value common sense, distrusting mystery.
(An onion helps resist the unknowing clouds,
each noxious whiff of teargas which obscures
or threatens to negate dissent.) What vital
issues we hold dear, think fit and decent
to debate, Enright's sharp wit and his clear-sighted
view of life and letters still illuminate.
He peeled the onions that he knew, and cared about,
and thus his criticism retains potency
over forty years and more, preserving all
its very pungent, necessary flavour.

AN ANCIENT ALUMNUS

His curtness seems curmudgeonly, sad echo of old rage.
Cured now of most current gossip, he's vexed at growing deaf.
Awkward, grim aloofness averts any mention of age,
and masks the resort to silence, an unvoiced fear of death.

'ON EARTH AS IT IS –'

In Heaven will there be escape
from creeping apathy, sly greed or rape?
None can explain *here* how it is
our God's called Property and *Hers* means *His*.

NOW AND THEN

Images blur, recur, grow sharper now and then,
slip into focus – teasing evidence of bliss,
significant events, keen educative strife.
Old memories endure, odd fragments of a life
difficult these days to construe, even convey.
Curiously, along with every test, one tries

to move through grey confines of age, dreamer's dismay,
and sometimes sift a modicum of truth from lies
during our vain quest for the new. Did yesterday
decay so fast, flesh become simply words? Will this
assembly of remembered times bridge some abyss
across the here and there, what passed for how and when?

SLOW LEARNING FUSE

They persist, these awkward questions that teach us all too late
how simple accidents of birth, strange circumstance,
affect each child.... It's not just lack of love and sense;
callous Authority's revered. We bow to Fame and Fate
or struggle to fit in, collude, sit smugly on the fence.
Masters of war endure meanwhile, inure our world to hate.